Invasive Species Takeover

ZEBRA MUSSELS

SCOTT PEARSON

Black Rabbit Books

Bolt is published by Black Rabbit Books
P.O. Box 3263, Mankato, Minnesota, 56002.
www.blackrabbitbooks.com
Copyright © 2017 Black Rabbit Books

Design and Production by Michael Sellner
Photo Research by Rhonda Milbrett

All rights reserved. No part of this book may be reproduced in any form without written permission from the publisher.

Library of Congress Control Number: 2015954919

HC ISBN: 978-1-68072-019-8   PB ISBN: 978-1-68072-283-3

Printed in the United States at CG Book Printers,
North Mankato, Minnesota, 56003. PO #1793 4/16

Web addresses included in this book were working and appropriate at the time of publication. The publisher is not responsible for broken or changed links.

Image Credits

Alamy: blickwinkel, 3, 20; blickwinkel/Hecker, 10; Dreamstime: Andrew Sabai, 24; Viter8, 31; Flickr: TownePost Network, 19; Getty: Peter Yates, 4–5; Newscom: Mark Hoffman/MCT, 32; Ron Offermans/Buiten-beeld/Minden Pictures, 28 (bottom); Public Domain: U.S. Fish & Wildlife Service, 14; Science Source: Ted Kinsman, 6; Scubaluna Photography: Flickr, Scubaluna Photography, Cover; Shutterstock: 1082492116, 28 (top); A_Lesik, 23 (bottom); Alex Kolokythas Photography, 13 (top); Anne Kitzman, 23 (top); sakhorn, 22; scubaluna, 27, 28 (middle); Vitalii Hulai, Back Cover, 1, 24–25, 8–9, 29
Every effort has been made to contact copyright holders for material reproduced in this book. Any omissions will be rectified in subsequent printings if notice is given to the publisher.

Contents

CHAPTER 1
Covered by Shells.....4

CHAPTER 2
Mussels on
the Move..............12

CHAPTER 3
Shells of
Destruction..........18

CHAPTER 4
Stopping Zebra
Mussels..............22

Other Resources...........30

CHAPTER 1

Covered by

Monroe, Michigan, had a problem. There was no running water. Without water, the power plant had to shut down. The people looked for answers. Soon, they found the main water pipe was clogged. It was full of shells.

5

Sticking to Everything

The shells belonged to zebra mussels. Zebra mussels are animals that live underwater. And they stick to anything. They make their homes on rocks or in pipes.

Zebra mussels also stick together. Thousands of mussels clump together in an area. These large groups easily clog pipes.

Some mussels even live on other animals.

THE ZEBRA MUSSEL UP CLOSE

SIPHONS

Invasive Species

The mussels in Monroe came from Lake Erie. But zebra mussels weren't supposed to be there. Several years ago, boats brought the mussels into U.S. lakes. These mussels spread to new areas. They hurt animals that already lived there. Zebra mussels are an **invasive species**.

CHAPTER 2

Mussels on the

Zebra mussels are from the Caspian and Black seas in **Eurasia**. Ships sailed in these seas. Then, the ships traveled across the ocean. The mussels came along. The first zebra mussels were discovered in the United States in 1988.

Spreading Fast

Birds and fish ate zebra mussels in Eurasia. They kept the mussel population low. But those **predators** weren't in North America. The mussels spread quickly. They hitched rides on boats. Then, they traveled to other lakes and rivers.

Zebra Mussels in U.S. Lakes

Today, zebra mussels live in about 700 out of 123,444 U.S. lakes.

WHERE ZEBRA MUSSELS ARE FOUND TODAY

Canada

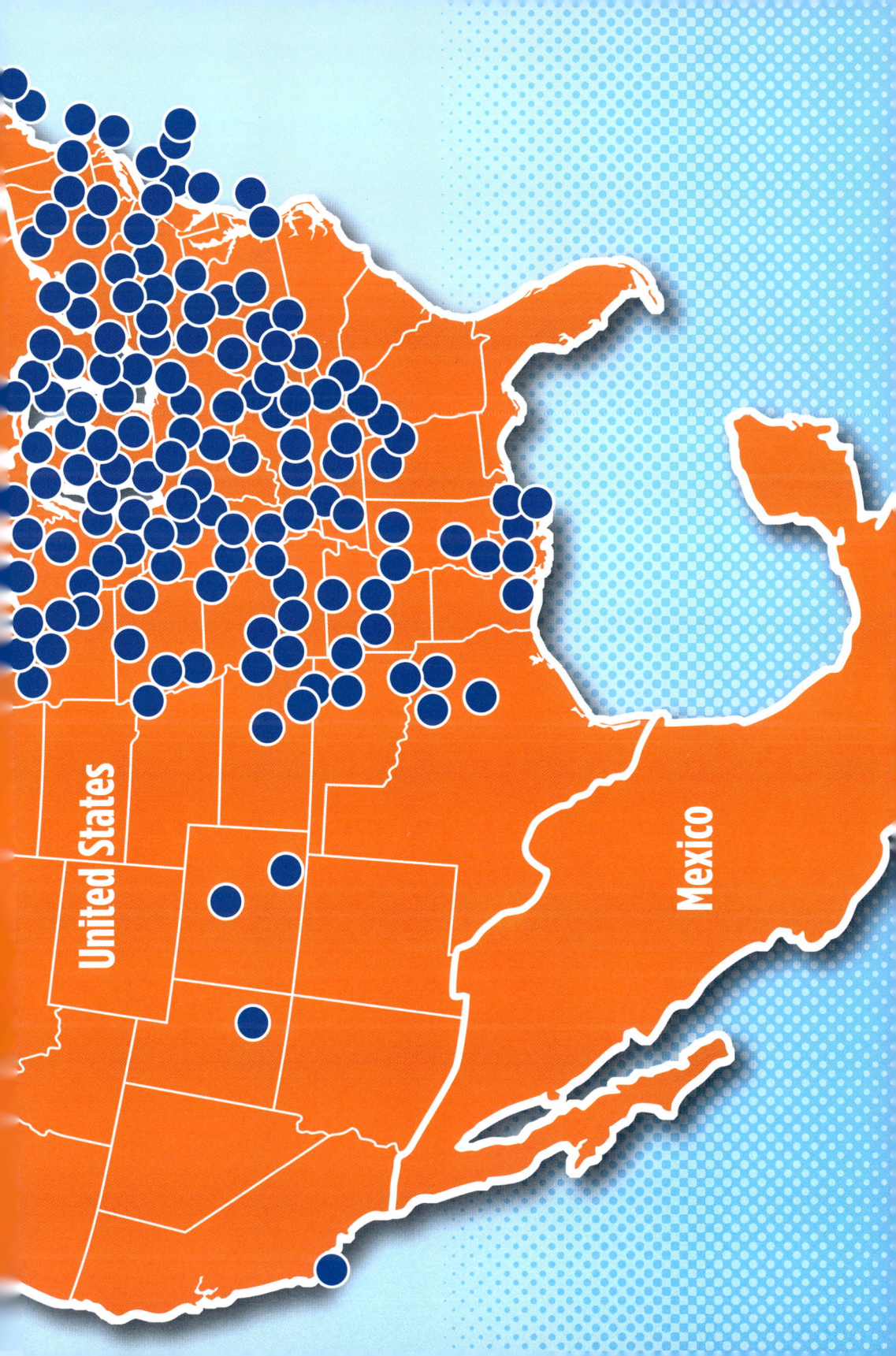

CHAPTER 3

Zebra mussels cause a lot of trouble. They get inside boat engines. Then, they clog them up. **Props** can get so covered with mussels they can't turn.

The mussels' shells are very sharp. They can easily cut a swimmer's foot.

Killed by Mussels

Zebra mussels also hurt other water animals. They will live right on top of other mussels. The mussels underneath can't open their shells. They starve to death.

Zebra mussels eat tiny plants in the water. This eating cleans the water. But it also takes food away from other animals.

CHAPTER 4

Stopping Zebra Mussels

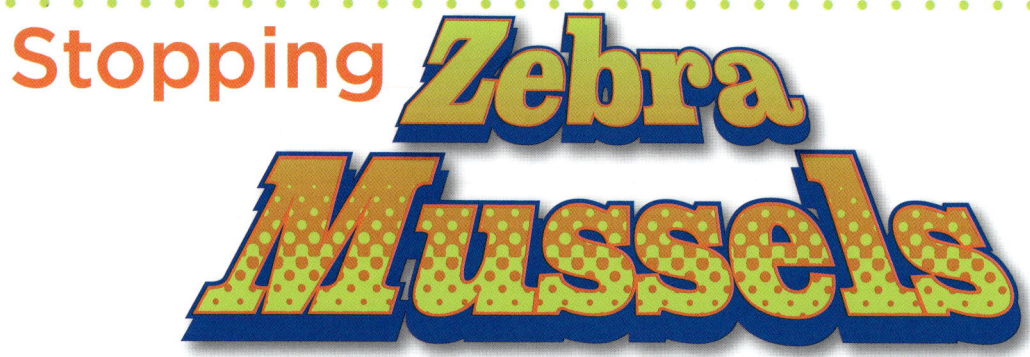

Zebra mussels usually get from place to place by sticking to boats. When a boat leaves the water, they stay on. When the boat is put into another lake, the mussels slide off.

To stop these riders, some states have passed laws. Boaters must check for mussels as they leave the water.

Cleaning Up after Boating

Search the boat for mussels.

Wash the boat with hot water.

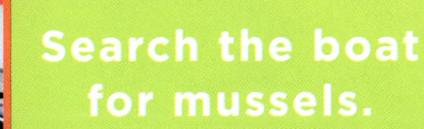

Throw bait away.

23

Getting Rid of Mussels

Some **chemicals** kill zebra mussels. But these chemicals also kill other animals. Scientists are trying to find a safe way to get rid of the mussels.

Zebra mussels can live out of water for more than a week.

Looking Forward

Zebra mussels are troublemakers. But they do a little good. They do help clean lake and river water. But without care, these creatures take over. That's why these invaders must be stopped.

27

ZEBRA MUSSELS BY THE NUMBERS

1 million
NUMBER OF EGGS A FEMALE LAYS IN A YEAR

2 years
AVERAGE LIFE SPAN

$5 BILLION
ESTIMATED AMOUNT SPENT TO STOP ZEBRA MUSSELS

10,000
NUMBER OF ZEBRA MUSSELS THAT CAN ATTACH TO ANOTHER MUSSEL

Think about It...

1. Chemicals kill zebra mussels. But many people don't want to use them. Use other sources to find out why chemicals might not be a good solution.

2. Boats carrying zebra mussels spread the creatures. How would you tell boaters about this problem?

3. What do you think should be done about zebra mussels? Use facts to support your answer.

GLOSSARY

byssus (BY-sus)—a strong, sticky thread that mussels use to attach themselves to surfaces

chemical (KE-muh-kuhl)—a substance that can cause a change in another substance

Eurasia (yur-AY-zhuh)—the two continents of Europe and Asia

invasive species (in-VAY-siv SPEE-seez)—animals or plants that spread through an area where they are not native, often causing problems for native plants and animals

predator (PRED-uh-tuhr)—an animal that eats other animals

prop (PRAHP)—a device with two or more blades that turns quickly to make a ship or aircraft move; prop is short for propeller.

siphon (SI-fun)—an organ used by mussels to suck in and then squirt out water

LEARN MORE

Kallio, Jamie. *12 Things to Know about Invasive Species.* Today's News. Mankato, MN: Peterson Pub. Co., 2015.

O'Connor, Karen. *The Threat of Invasive Species.* Animal 911: Environmental Threats. New York: Gareth Stevens Publishing, 2014.

Spilsbury, Richard. *Invasive Species Underwater.* Invaders from Earth. New York: PowerKids Press, 2015.

WEBSITES

Alien Profile: Zebra Mussel
dnr.wi.gov/org/caer/ce/eek/critter/invert/zebramussel.htm

Frequently Asked Questions about the Zebra Mussel
fl.biology.usgs.gov/Nonindigenous_Species/Zebra_mussel_FAQs/zebra_mussel_faqs.html

Zebra Mussel
www.dnr.state.mn.us/invasives/aquaticanimals/zebramussel/index.html

INDEX

B

body parts, 8–9

D

damage, 4, 7, 18, 21

E

eggs, 28

F

food, 21

I

introduction to nonnative areas, 11, 12, 15

L

life span, 28

S

stopping spread, 22–23, 25